Trapped! Was It Really God?

Earlina Gilford-Weaver

Trapped: Earlina Gilford-Weaver

Although the author and publisher have made every effort to ensure that the information in this book was correct at press time, the author and publisher (Maximize Publishing Inc. & Dr. Michael McCain) do not assume and hereby disclaim any liability to any party for any loss, damage, or disruption caused by errors or omissions, whether such errors or omissions result from negligence, accident, or any other cause.

The names and identifying characteristics of certain individuals referenced in this publication have been changed. This publication contains the opinions and ideas of its author.

No warranty is made with respect to the accuracy or completeness of the information contained herein, and both the author and publisher specifically disclaim any responsibility for any liability, loss, or risk, personal or otherwise, which is incurred as a consequence, directly or indirectly, of the use and application of any of the contents of this book.

Maximize Publishing Inc.

2018 Monterey Ave

Bronx N.Y. 10457

Attn.: Michael McCain

C/o: Kevin Brown

© 2014 by Maximize Publishing Inc. & Earlina Gilford-Weaver

All rights reserved, including the right to reproduce this book

Trapped: Earlina Gilford-Weaver

Or portions thereof in any form whatsoever. Any Reproduction of this book in recording, print or otherwise is punishable by law and copy right standards. For any information or contact with the author you may write the above named address.

ISBN-13:
978-0692201756 (Maximize Publishing Inc.)

ISBN-10:
0692201750

Trapped: Earlina Gilford-Weaver

Trapped! Was It Really God?

Earlina Gilford-Weaver

Trapped: Earlina Gilford-Weaver

Table Of Contents:

Forward……………………………………………………9

Trapped Was It Really God?...13

Knock At The Door…………………………………………..29

The Next Day……………………………………………………45

Pastors Office…………………………………………………49

Knock Knock…………………………………………………...53

Pastors Office Again……………………………………………65

Two Weeks Later- Donna & Donnie's Apartment…………69

Saturday, The Birthday Party……………………………………..73

One Hour Later…………………………………………………..87

Six Months Later……………………………………………105

Pop Questions……………………………………………117

Trapped: Earlina Gilford-Weaver

Forward

Dr. Michael McCain

"Trapped" was it really God? One of the most breath taking stories I have ever read. A family who seems to have it all together or the exterior but struggling with skeletons and bones in the closct; this loving yet dysfunctional family has some deep rooted secrets that would destroy sisterhood, parenthood and marriages. Through the pages of this book you will discover how one family deals with the reality of the bones in their closet the dysfunction that is being uncovered and the healing that needs to be brought forth.

This story will shake the hearts of the feeble, so brace yourself. This story will open your eyes to learning forgiveness in hard places and learning some of the secrets that sometimes remain hidden in marriages that appear to be perfect. Earlina Gilford-Weaver is a gifted an anointed author who's message transcends the pews of the church to reach a real and right now generation. Her message, her voice, her ministry will impact this 21st. century in a powerful way. Roll your sleeves up and see where your heart takes you in this thriller entitled, "Trapped"…

Trapped: Earlina Gilford-Weaver

Trapped: Earlina Gilford-Weaver

Trapped! Was It Really God?

In some families we often think that it could never happen to us when we hear of others that go through such secrets that could never come knocking at my door, but in this circle of deceits, secrets, and wanting to be with someone because we just don't want to be alone God had to give this man to me, but in the mirror i say was it Really God?
A Story that hit a small town in Ohio that we only see on a Life Time Movie,
It can't happen to a well-known Christian family,
But when it do, how do we find forgiveness and recover from the shock, shame and blame?

I would like to thank my Lord & Savior for allowing me to write these short stories that
Brings the real in our today life's, that are funny, exciting, and healing for the

Trapped: Earlina Gilford-Weaver

Christian & Non-Christian life style.
Special Thank you to My Husband Richard A. Weaver
My Children Theresa, Floyd & Jermaine
My Grandchildren, Shekinah, Manuel, Braylin, Sayvion, Nevaeh
Special Thank you to Shekinah Glory Drama Team

All my short stories are turn into Gospel Stage Plays!!!
For Events dates & clippings go to
www.shekinahglorydrama.com

TRAPPED! Was It Really God?

Chapter 1

Lord' this marriage is a joke, Donnie is never home, and it seems like he is with another woman, I truly hate to believe this but why don't Donny touch me like he use to? Why he do not say he loves me like he use to? I know he took on more at his job, but that is no reason because I have a lot on my plate as well and still come home to cook his dinner and tell him I love him, I truly need a friend to talk to' let me call Carol, I am about to lose my mind, Carol can you please come over right now, we need to talk! *"Knock, Knock. Knock"*

My God Carol what did you do catch a jet? I only ask for you to come, no hard feelings Charlene, but I am going through something
Well I asked her Donna because you said it was between life and death and I believe it's these new shoes I ordered last week from Step in a flash.com, that made me run to Charlene house to have her bring me here, so

Trapped: Earlina Gilford-Weaver

tell me what is the juicy news you got to tell me?
Pause...

Hold that thought let me put my phone on vibrate I can't miss a word.
I am sorry Donna, but Carol said it was an emergency, and asked me to give her a ride, and you know what the word of God says, where there is two or three gathered in my name I am in the mist, so Donna you did say you needed me in a flash and since Charlene was the best option that could fly me over here with her police chopper, I told her that you were about blow up the bank and share the money with me and I was going to give her a cut, you know when you tell black folks it is money involved, you can get curb side service, so what is the juicy news, you found me a new man?

Girl stop it, I just needed a friend to talk too, because Donnie is driving me crazy, 1year and 9 month s of being his wife, and it feels like 50 years, he is barley home he never touch me like he did when we first start dating or when we got married, and it has truly got me so concerned about my marriage.

Trapped: Earlina Gilford-Weaver

Girl I know what you mean, you have been looking and acting more and more like an old woman, maybe it is them grandma pajamas you be wearing,
Donna I can leave so you two can talk in private and I will be praying for you and Donnie.

Thanks a lot Carol, but no Charlene it fine please stay I need another level head advice, and you have been married a little longer than I have, and I truly do need a word from the lord. And you right where there is two together in the name of Jesus,
Wait a minute Donna what are you trying to say? it is three of us one two three I know you are stress out but I hope your vision is still good, and you know me, I love keeping it real, Charlene is too old' what she knows about young love, now on the other hand I can tell you a lot.

Well Carol since you like keeping it real, give me some real sister to sister advice,
On that friend of yours Donnie, I truly believe that I made the wrong decision on walking down the aisle and saying I do too soon.

"Why would you say that"?

Trapped: Earlina Gilford-Weaver

Girl I looked good walking down that aisle with my sexy red low cut butte tight fitted dress, and girl did you see how people was checking out my new walk, all you haters was hating on me, so no the time was just right while I still have this delicious hot body before this lucky man knocked me up.

Carol stay focus this is not about that messed up walk that almost messed up my wedding day, and this is not about you today, I am truly thinking about getting a divorce attorney, I am really not sure if this marriage was in God's plan for me, or was it just another one of my bad choices, I really don't think God sent this man for me.

Donna if I can say something, maybe you guys need Christian marriage counseling, I have been married to Brother Devon for 7 years now and it was rough at first, but they do say the first five years are the hardest, but it will get better if you keep God in it.

What! 5 years are you crazy, that is too long for me, if Donnie don't get it together in 5 more months then I'll kick his behind to the curve, oh wait a minute' Girl you got to hang in there, don't give up yet, the last time I watched divorce court which was when you call me, and

Trapped: Earlina Gilford-Weaver

I had to pause my TV, that child did not get anything, because they had to be married for at least 5 years just to receive the family car, girl we cannot go back to riding in style in a Pinto, I look too good for that' the devil is a lie and the truth is not in him!

News flash Carol you just rode in one with me on the way over here.
Is that what it was? Well no one saw me in that, because she was doing 250miles to get here.

Carol you need to quit, this is not about possessions, I am not happy' material things can not heal or fix what my heart feels, Donnie is always gone, 1year and 9 months and I only seen my husband 5 times in our bed, but in the beginning we spent lots of time together, now all we do when we do see each other is fuss and fight, we stop praying together, reading the bible together, we don't even go to church any more together, I believe in my heart he is cheating on me.

Well check this out girl' I got this new tracking device on I got your behind now.com, I ordered it after this girl on Perry Wringer show found her man in a blink of an eyelid, she found his butt naked behind fast, so If you

Trapped: Earlina Gilford-Weaver

need to you can borrow it I can lend it to you for a loan of five hundred dollars.

Donna I just cannot believe Donnie would ever cheat on you, that man loves and adores you, maybe it's his job' sometimes that can stress a man believe me,
Charlene give me a break, work, stress the word of God does tells us that if a man don't work he don't lay, I believe it is because he has to many woman to provide for with just that one job, they man needs three, since he got three women to take care of.

I thought so Charlene, but he tells me his business is great, but the late night calls are getting out of control, I tried talking to him about us getting counseling, but he gets crazy and don't want to hear it saying he has no issues maybe it's just me and Carol the word of God says if a man don't work then he can't eat., and wait a minute what do you mean Carol he got to take care of three women?

Do I have to teach you everything? let me refresh your memory when we were kids we said that whosoever get married first will always look after each other, so he has you right?
"Right"

Trapped: Earlina Gilford-Weaver

Your mama Right?
"Right"
And me that three 1-2-3, but we can stop the checks for your mama that will free him up for 2 more night in the bed, and I know you cook good as a chef so we know that is not the issue, you keep the house clean so we know that's not the problem, so maybe I can talk to him, you know he was my boy toy before you guys got together, having all this body girl must of worn that man out.
Carol you got some very serious issues, Donna would you like for me to pray for you guys and maybe anoint the house?

I am just playing, have some sense of humor Charlene because I had Devon too
Yes I believe that in your dreams.
Yes you got that right in his dreams and yours too, but Donna you know Donnie is like a brother to me, I was the one who introduce you two, let me see where his head at before you make a bad decision that will affect us all.
What does my decision got to do with you Carol? I know you love us both, but it should not affect your life.

Trapped: Earlina Gilford-Weaver

Donna have you seen Donnie friends lately? Girl please' that would affect me a lot, they all are fine and have big bank accounts, remember the one I met at you guys wedding? Ed he melt my weave right off my hair with his fine self, until his fat wife found out, after his kids told I was stalking their school and house, I just knew that man was my soul mate.

Wait a minute… you said Will was your soul mate, when you met him at me and Devon engagement party, I thought he was love at first sight' your soul mate. Well Charlene you know the word better than I do, the good word says that the first shall be last and the last shall be first, so do the subtraction.
Girl you crazy, but I did need some laughs right about now, I truly thank you both for stopping by, and Charlene you right maybe me and Donnie need some Christian Counseling I will call Minister Knight and make an appointment, let's all go to the spa I need a pamper me day, my treat.

So are you guys saying my relationships are a joke? All I am saying girl you better think twice about a divorce, I can't go back to the free for a second time, at the Y.Y.C.A.

Trapped: Earlina Gilford-Weaver

You said it not me, Carol' but seriously I care less about how much money Donnie has, or what he does for me because what I am going through never comes with a price tag, the last time I read the word of God, Peace, Love and Unity in my marriage is what I need not a check with a break down.

Well since you talking about divorcing Donnie let's go shopping, and put everything at my house before Donnie closes all the credit cards or you go broke on an Attorney.
Carol what do shopping got to do with me divorcing Donnie?
You see Donna you don't listen, 6 months verse 5 years, girl you will be broke, so let's get our money worth while we can, do the math, do the math, I thought you had a degree or two.

Girl you are a hot mess, I did not say I was divorcing Donnie today or if I am going too, let us go.
Amen, you guys go ahead, I got to drop off the police car and I will caught you both later , and Donna please make that appointment with the Pastor for the counseling believe me it works.
You guys are killing me I was just saying, No man know what time or hour the bank might close, you know

Trapped: Earlina Gilford-Weaver

the word, that's in the bible, I heard Pastor Little preach that sermon last week when I was visiting my cousin church looking for my new man.
Lord please touch your child in the name of Jesus.

Later that night:

"**Donna talking on the phone**" Hello mother, how are you today? Yes I got the letter from her yesterday, she will not be here for another month, Yes Donnie is still at work, yes mother, yes mother, see you tomorrow.
"**Donnie walks in the door**"
Every time I walk in the door you are always on the phone running them chops, maybe you need a job as a telemarketing.
Hello Donnie' and baby that was mother on the phone, and how was my man day?
What she want now? More money again? Maybe I should have married her' they do say it is cheaper to keep her.

Now Donnie was that nice to say? And no she called to see when her granddaughter was coming home from college. It is around that time for Precious to come home.
I hope never, that girl of yours is nothing but trouble, she better been glad I am not her father, she acts like

22

Trapped: Earlina Gilford-Weaver

that nasty sister of yours, I thought it was her child when we first met, I guess personality can fool you.

Now you can say whatever you like Donnie' but that's my child, so drop the attitude concerning mine, I don't know why you don't like Precious, she never done anything to you but respect you as a father, it is sad that you feel that way about her, But can we please have a peaceful night together?
We can if I can come home for once and see my wife in something sexy, and not running them chops on the phone all the time and them grandma pajamas, and what's for dinner? Conversation' it seems like that all you can make lately.
I am going to ignore what you just said Donnie and get dinner.

"Knock knock" Donnie answer door"
Hey man what's up? What bring you this way tonight?
Man Donnie its Lisa, That woman is driving me up a wall' she is talking about she might be pregnant,
Melvin I told you to put that chick on a leash, the day you met her crazy behind.
Man I had to leave and get some air, the last thing we need is a child, the way she acts' she acts like one herself, all ways talking about baby can I have this, baby

Trapped: Earlina Gilford-Weaver

can I have that' Baby my hair' baby my nails, baby, baby, baby man I can't get no rest, Donnie is Donna like that too?

Yeah right she knows better and like I told you before as long as you keep paying all the bills, I would not give her a but time, her behind would work for it, I told you when you met her she is nothing but a high price gold digging hole, by the way let me tell you a secret' she tried to hit on me.

Yeah right' Donnie, you are not Lisa type, believe that You got that right' I am not a dame fool.

Man you know what the good book say, the man is the provider, and to treat his wife as he would himself, so the sky is the limit for my queen, she got to look good if I look good, so that do not make me a fool, so chill about the nasty comments, that is my wife.
man she got you more than wet behind the ear, you drowning in the brain' Donna knows not to try that mess with me, that's why I test the water before I said I do, maybe you should follow the real man steps on how to keep his woman in check,

Trapped: Earlina Gilford-Weaver

Whatever man, where is Donna anyway? I truly don't understand how you got her to agree to marry your crazy behind.

She knew I was the best thing she ever came across and she is in there doing what a good natural wife do, cooking her king some dinner.
Then what happen to her sister? Lisa can't cook a toast without burning it up, just the other day I asked her to make me a sandwich, and she went outside and got a cup of sand, and asked me which way I want it.
Ha… ha… ha… man that's why you take it on a test ride before you say I do, take it on the freeway and see how well it ride, beauty sometimes don't come with brains, she got you man ha… ha… ha… a cup of sand, man you got issues.

Well I guess your cup runs over, because Donna has beauty, brains and can cook, so I see you doing well in that department.
Don't hate because I got it like that.

Well tell my favorite Sis-in-law to keep up the good work, I never thought anyone could settle you down,

Trapped: Earlina Gilford-Weaver

and make an honest man out of you, especially a woman! If you know what I mean'
Keep your voice down man, Donna knows nothing about my past, and all things change nothing stays the same, for all she knows I am a church boy, so chill man ...what!

Donnie that's something you don't keep from your wife man, and you would not know Jesus if he was standing right next to you.

And you think you do? That is why you whipped now; I bet you believe Lisa is Mary,
Whatever man I check you later, Lisa is waiting on me I told her I was going to the store.
Oh by the way you got any pregnancy tests?
Melvin what do I need a pregnancy test for? And what you need one for? I know Lisa is not trying to give upon sharing your money.

Man every time I hit that she screams I think I'm pregnant, and send me to the store for a pregnant test,
Man like I said you got some serious issues, Donna knows not to play them games, she knows we will never have a child, and you better not have said anything about my past to that big mouth wife of yours either.

Trapped: Earlina Gilford-Weaver

No man, your gigolo male prostitute life style safe with me, and plus that's your demon to carry. You should man' Donna is a Queen and want a child with you, so what are you waiting for.

Like I said man you got issues, later "Melvin walks out the door"
"Donna walks in room"
Honey who was here? I heard you in here talking to someone.
Is my Dinner done? And that was Melvin' he stopped by to see if we had a pregnancy test, you know your sister got issues, I know you better not try that mess with me
What! She Pregnant? She never said anything to me or ma when we went out to lunch earlier. I got to call Lisa, that's some great news if she is.
Really I don't know, and don't care, you know how your family are' they would make a rock into a mountain, and plus Melvin is not too far from the branches, you sure he is not your brother?
Whatever Donnie, you know we are good women, that's why you married me, and Melvin is a good Husband and brother-in-law maybe you could earn something from him.

Trapped: Earlina Gilford-Weaver

If you say so, I'm tired, I am about to go to bed you coming?
What about dinner honey?
Bring it in the room to your king' I'm about to go and take a shower, so fix your man up the way I like it.
"Walks away"
Lord I feel like I am on a roller coaster ride, sometimes my marriage is up and sometimes it's down, I feel like my husband don't love me sometimes, did he really marry me because he loved me or was it because of what I could do for him? I feel trapped, did you give this husband to me lord or was it just my flesh feeling lonely?

"Knock At The Door"
Chapter 2

Hello mother' what brings you this way?
Donna do a mother need a reason to stop by and see her child? What you doing anyway, you should be glad to see me since that no good father of yours don't come or call.

No mame' you do not need a reason to stop by and you are looking very nice today,
Where is my favorite son-in-law? With his fine self, you know if I was a couple of years younger, child I would give you a run for your money, and snatch Donnie sexy Vanilla tall slim big feet straight from you.

Mother' get a hold of yourself' Donnie is at work, and I was just about to leave so that I can stop by Lisa home on my way paying bills, Melvin stop by last night and told Donnie that he thinks Lisa might be pregnant, I hope she is we need a new bundle of joy, don't you think so mother?
Who could Lisa be pregnant by?

Trapped: Earlina Gilford-Weaver

Her husband mother, who else.

Well I am just asking, you know how lose your sister is, that child change men like I change my wigs, and you know how many I go through a day, by the way did Donnie leave that check for mama? I am about due a new hairdo. **"Touching her wig"**.

Yes mother, here it goes, and what is it that my husband got going on with my mother, that he give you checks every week? And I got to beg for gas money' Like he is paying some type of child support or something? You get more than I do, I know since daddy left you needed a little support from us but this is getting ridiculous.

Don't hate, appreciate that you have a man like Donnie, that cares for your mother, a lot of son-in-laws care less like that little sissy your sister married too, and you know mama got it like that' Donnie is a good **"pause looking at the check"** **wow!** A great son-in-law, don't give that man any lip, he takes good care of you, not like that bum you were dating in college, he could care less, you could not even afford to buy your mama a early hop breakfast, so God had to remove that hot mess and bless us with a gold mine.

Trapped: Earlina Gilford-Weaver

Ma what kind of thinking is that? And Jason was a very deceit, caring, loving, loyal young man, that loved the lord, and was working two jobs to pay his way through med school, and material things and money can never replace true love, and you know we would of got married if Jason was not killed by that drunk driver, how in the world could you or would you compare my lost to riches?

Well it just might help Donna, you always was weak like your daddy a fool, never know what a good thing is, but know when you got money the love grows even better when a man satisfies his woman financially and sexually, you got it made, that's why your daddy had to go, Mama needed her groove back if you know what I mean.

Thank God I do not think the way you do, and who said I have all what you think I need?
Just look all around you Donna' are you blind or crazy like your daddy?
Mother no matter how much Donnie provides, it is not enough if I am still starving for the love, affection, peace and touch of a husband, believe me money is not worth losing all the above, and daddy is not a fool he loves us.

Trapped: Earlina Gilford-Weaver

Well I tried showing you all my tricks' on how to keep a man satisfy, the way he needs to be, but you had to consult God! And wait until you were married, so now you don't know what or how Donnie really needs & how he likes it, just like your daddy never knew how to keep me.

And you know how Donnie likes it Mother?
Donna you are talking crazy Donnie is not enough man for me, that's why he has you.
If it was not for them checks Donnie was giving you every week you would have talked about him the same way you do every guy we ever dated.
Child you better be glad I just got my nails done, you most forgot who I am, Mrs. Donna Louise Patricia Williams.

Let's go Mother 'it is no need of talking to you, thank God daddy took us to church and taught us some type of values, this is why I can't talk to you and I do turn to God all the time, I have no one else to look up too since you ran daddy away.

Yes Lord we better end this conversation right now before I lose my own respect I got for me and Stop,

Trapped: Earlina Gilford-Weaver

Drop, and Roll on that behind, don't get it twisted and forget that you are my child and I will put you back where the Lord made you from, The Dust.
Sorry ma, but you have a strange "pause" I mean unique way of laying down the foundation of what a wife need to please her husband, and what a husband need to please his wife, but I love you any way. Let's go see Lisa this will give us all a pleasant morning

Yes, you better get it right' and know that I am the reason Donnie is still here, but you go ahead I got to go pick your little sister up from day care, and go cash this check while it is still hot, "giving mother a hug both walks out door"

"Later that evening"

"Donna, Carol, Charlene all sitting on couch" My God it has been a long day, I went by my sister house, because I had got some good news last night and needed to ask her about it, but could not find her, and my mother stopped over this morning to pick up her weekly allowance Donnie gives her, and girl just let me tell you my mother Mrs. Pat Ozzie Renee Pearl McBride is a hot mess.

Trapped: Earlina Gilford-Weaver

Girl you are preaching to the choir, I know how Mrs. McBride gets down. Wait a minute did you just say Donnie gives her a weekly allowance, what is that all about, and where is mine?

Really, that is awesome Donnie does that because my Devon gives his mother money every pay since his father died, he feels a widow should be helped out time to time, that's what Minister Knight said in her sermon a few months ago, and since your father is not around maybe Donnie feels that would make you feel better to look after your mother.

Wait a minute Charlene and Donna I second motion that, Mrs. McBride is not Donnie Mother' nor his child, how much she gets girl?
Carol he gives my mother a large piece of change, and gives me a monthly dew drop saying I make enough' he got his priorities messed up if you ask me, and Charlene I don't mine my husband looking out for my mother don't get me wrong but more than he gives his wife. That's crazy, wait a minute maybe I can get ex girlfriend support, hey how much will I get? I am talking to you Charlene, since you are the head in charge of giving widow mama's.com.

Trapped: Earlina Gilford-Weaver

Stop day dreaming Carol' Donnie and you never ever dated and maybe you need to help your mother out sometimes.
When hell' gets hotter, and what is this news you were saying concerning your sister Donna? You know Lisa **"Knock knock"**.

Hold that thought Carol **"walks over to answer door"**
Carol the saying is' when hell freezes over.
I know what I said Carlene, and I what I meant, so stop playing professor check a homie.

Hello sis what is the emergency you said you need to ask me? Leaving note pad paper all over my door for everyone to read, and blowing up my phone.
Well hello to you too Lisa, and where have you been? I came by your Apartment, The nail shop, hair salon, and the spa looking for you.
I was shopping for a new wardrobe Donna, what is it? Someone died?
Well Lisa I heard.
Heard what Donna? Come on spill the beans.

Allow me to finish Lisa, I don't want to be rude and ask you with everyone here.

Trapped: Earlina Gilford-Weaver

Why not? They are always here, their like a piece of your furniture that is too heavy to move or replace, so spit it out, oh by the way hello ladies, it must be juicy I see you all are here. For a minute I had to pitch myself and Charlene to see if I was visible, when you did not speak Mrs. Lisa.

Hello Lisa you are looking very nice today
Well I am sorry I do have better manners than to speak to my elders, and thank you Charlene I always look good, so sis what is this news you need to ask me, chasing me all over town. Melvin came by last night and told Donnie that he thought you was pregnant, and asked us for a pregnancy test.

What! Shut the front, back and side door, Melvin finally got a touchdown and tacked that butt for once. I know I did not hear you right, and Carol you can shut every door of your mouth because I am not, Why did Melvin tell Donnie that mess? I am not pregnant' Donnie had to hear that wrong, No he heard him right, because he asked Donnie did we have a pregnancy test around the house.

Girl please I will not mess up this hot, Delicious, sexy body for no one, I just tell him that when we are making

Trapped: Earlina Gilford-Weaver

love, so he can hit it harder' it boost up his man hood, so when he think he has done something big, he gives me a bigger allowance to fills up my closet more, you know what I mean Carol. No sweetie I don't know what you mean, because if I ever screamed out them words my man would get up and run. Just like Donnie.

Lisa you are your mother's child, you had to get that trick from mother, you better stop crying wolf before you get caught, God is no one to play with and if your husband would like a family you should want to have his child he is a good man, and Carol Donnie do not run, we are just waiting until the time is right.

Well guys you can stop planning a baby shower unless the cloths size is a 4 petite **"taking pills out her purse"** I am supplied enough and never will get caught, and don't you even think about saying anything to Donnie you tell him too much as is Donna.
Well you guys I got to get going, some of us do work, call me later Donna about the party you are planning that we talked about for your baby sister
Okay Charlene have a bless day and drive careful out there.

Trapped: Earlina Gilford-Weaver

Drive careful, she is the police so what she need to be care for, they better be careful of her driving, the other day I seen my life, your life and everybody else life flash across my hair when I almost lost some of my braids on the way over here, I am telling you Charlene is a undercover ride by chick.
Bye half pint of a brain, see you guys later "walking out the door"

I am so glad she is gone, I wanted to express my vision on her new look she has, did anyone notice?
What new look Carol? Charlene looks the same to me, That is what I am saying we have been going to the spa, gym, and those hips of hers seem to be getting wider than that truck she drives, Devon must be knocking every corner, truly I don't see how he never was good in knocking my boots, 1 second and the boy is knocked out, so Lisa back to the baby talk now that Charlene is gone we can get the truth. You are so crazy Carol I never knew you dated Brother Devon, and there is no baby talk this way! Carol never dated Brother Devon, stop playing around Carol someone might really take that serious.

Who playing Donna, please I had Donnie, Melvin, Devon, and Minister Knight

Trapped: Earlina Gilford-Weaver

Now that's nasty, you had a woman too?
No Lisa Mr. Knight her husband, am strictly sticky all a woman can do for me is move aside and let me have her man.

Lord, deliver this child in Jesus name, but Lisa for real stop playing games with your husband you have a good one, and he deserves to be a father' plus I was kind of excited if you were, a niece, nephew, or twins would be nice to have in the family.

Well Donna get over your day dreaming, I really thought you had some awesome news to say like Daddy died and we have a large Insurance policy to cash. Jesus, Jesus, **"scratching her head"** I think I had him too, but anyway Donna when are you and Donnie going to have me a Godchild? Don't you think it is about that time since we are talking about babies and you are not getting any younger?

Well Carol it does sound good, but Donnie is not ready, he gets upset if I even think or say the word baby, girl even when I call him baby' just hearing the name he acts like a fool, but I am praying that he will come around soon I would like a child with my husband and

Trapped: Earlina Gilford-Weaver

Precious is turning 18 now, and is away in college but after 18 years I hope my body can handle it again.

Well sis I do have bags tricks that would make that man change his mind if you know what I mean, why do you think Melvin screams baby every time he get a little. Well we all know that she is Mrs. Pat McBride product, if you know what I mean.

Lisa, I am praying for you, just give me a call later, I wanted us to go over the plans for our new found sister mother adopted after that long trip she took down to the Virgin Island, and Destiny will be turning one years old this weekend, I don't know what it did to mother after daddy leaving her after my wedding had her leave for a year and come back with a new born baby girl very odd. Yes it was very strange to leave right after daddy walked out on her.

I ask myself every day what happened to our parents, but that trip mom took did do her some good, maybe that was what she needed to fill a void, that's why she had to adopt a child, but why after 30 years, but why a 1 month old? When she got to change diapers and start all over again, well it has been 1 year since that happened and our little sister will be one years old, thank God she

Trapped: Earlina Gilford-Weaver

came home with a cute baby, because them African kids look rough, you watch, CET.

Lisa girl you are crazy' I thought she got the baby from the Virgin Islands?
It was the Virgin Islands Carol' and Lisa them kids need help and all God creation is beautiful, well enough we need to do something special for that day.
Yeah if anyone did not know your family, they would believe she was your real sister because she looks just like you Donna.

I tell her that all the time, mother picked out a twin in a baby kind of way.
Whatever you guys, should we invite daddy? I don't even know if he knows about Destiny, I have not even seen him or talked to him since the wedding, he said it is too hard to be around us right now because if he told us why he really left it would destroy our whole family.

That just sounds crazy, he will not even return any of my calls either, I cannot believe it had anything to do with us, maybe we need to ask mother why he left'
Maybe it was another woman, daddy loved us to much just to walk out like he did, he owes me well us an

Trapped: Earlina Gilford-Weaver

explanation, and it has been hard on me to count on Melvin for all my financial needs.

Well Lisa asking mother is like talking to a wall, every time you bring his name up' she go crazy, any way call me tonight both of you, I got to get dinner started before Donnie gets home and see you guys here and smell no food, it would only makes things worse, that man be hungry when he gets home.

Okay love you Mrs. Chef Wife-Ardee, I wished you had it all cooked by now so I could surprise Melvin, that man would of gave me a big allowance thinking I learned how to cook just for him, I need a new outfit for this party this week-end, but better you than me, Melvin cooks, clean' and do the final dessert touch up on this sexy, delicious body of mine.

Well you can throw down in the kitchen Donna, and Lisa why do you need a new outfit to a one year old birthday party? Just wear some jeans and tee-shirt, with all them babies there cake and ice cream I would not wear my Sunday best.
Carol that's why you don't have a man, you got to look sexy at all times no matter what the occasion is and I

Trapped: Earlina Gilford-Weaver

cannot allow a bunch one two or three year old to out shine me.

Lisa you are a hot mess this party is not a fashion show this is a day for us to show our mother that we support her having Destiny.

Ha ha ha, let's go I will walk out with you Lisa, I want to see that new car I heard you just got, call me later Donna if you want me to help out too.
"Hugs then they walk out door".

Lord help them both slave and slave-master, let me get this dinner started before my husband gets home, and put something on sexy and show Donnie I still have this sexy body, who knows I might just get lucky and make a Donnie or Donna Jr.

Trapped: Earlina Gilford-Weaver

"The Next day"

Chapter 3

"**Donna talking on phone**" Hello Melvin, have you seen Donnie? He did not come home last night, did you guys work overnight? Okay, thank you, I will call you soon as he gets in. "**Hangs up the phone**" Lord …Lord… what is going on? I pray nothing happened, this is not like Donnie to not come home "**Knock on door**" maybe that's Donnie but why would he knock and not use his key "**answer door**" Oh It's you, Hello Brother Devon what brings you here this morning?

Praise the Lord Sister Donna, how are you on this bless day? I was over this way to stop by to visit a sick member of the church and decided to come by and pick up some things Donnie mention he had, I hope that was okay' Is everything fine?
Yes Brother Devon, everything thing is great, why would you ask

Trapped: Earlina Gilford-Weaver

You just look distance or something heavy on your mind Sister, Well I talked with Brother Donnie a few days ago and told him that I would stop bye to pick up some old clothing he has to donate to the brotherhood outreach, is he here? I know he don't work on Saturdays.

No Brother Devon, I believe he left already for the gym, when I woke up he was already gone, I really don't know about the clothes, but as so soon as Donnie gets in I will have him call you, I hate you drove all the way across town, but I don't want to give you the wrong clothes. That's okay my sister, I was in the neighborhood, just have Brother Donnie to call me later today and I will come right over, are you sure everything okay? You look very worried about something Sister Donna.

Everything is fine, Brother Devon I was just thinking about the shopping for my little sister birthday party next week that's all, making sure I have everything covered.
Oh how old will Destiny be? She has gotten so big and walking already
She will be 1 years old, and yes she started walking very fast before her time.

Trapped: Earlina Gilford-Weaver

I had almost forgot that Mrs. McBride had adopted a child, that is a bless thing to do, giving a child a chance of a better wonderful life.

Yes Brother Devon we are so bless to have Destiny in our life's, everyone say she looks like me when I was a baby, mother met Destiny mother when she went to the Virgin Island and the young lady could not care for her and was putting her up for adoption, so mother stayed until after the birth and adopted her and brought her to the states when Destiny was just 2 weeks old.

What a Blessings' so when are you guys planning to have the party?

Well this Saturday at the fellowship hall, we really want to surprise our mother me and Lisa to show her we truly proud of her adopting Destiny at her age.
Well I know Mrs. McBride will be very please well I better be going maybe me and Steffie will bring Devon Jr you know he will be that terrible three in a couple of months.
That will be awesome we would love for you guys to bring him to have cake and ice cream with the birthday girl.

Trapped: Earlina Gilford-Weaver

Well let your husband know' I stopped by, and Sister Donna you have bless day.

You too Brother Devon, and I when Donnie gets in I will be sure to let him know you stopped by for the donations of the clothes. **"Brother Devon walks out door" Donnie picks up phone makes call to Donnie"** Donnie this is me, honey I am concern, you have not called me back, I have left 7 messages, please give me a call, I am getting very concern. **"hang up phone"** Lord I am depending on you to give me a word a sign or something to let me know that Donnie is okay, what is going on Lord I know Donnie would not mess up our marriage by being with another woman, could he Lord?

"Pastors Office"
Chapter 4

Good morning Pastor Knight how long have you been here?
Good morning Brother Devon, little over an hour, it is good to see you here as well, I came by to surprise you all by getting things ready for the brotherhood luncheon, you guys need a little woman touch, Pastor do cook, so I came a little early to bless you all with a special treat of mine.

Well Thank you Pastor, can't wait to taste your blessing again, and I stopped by Brother Donnie home to pick up the clothes he wanted to donate to the shelter, but was not able to retrieve them, because he was not there, that brother has some sharp stuff, and gives some nice things to the men shelter all the time, I got a couple of sweaters from him myself.

Trapped: Earlina Gilford-Weaver

Yes, that Brother Donnie does give awesome things to the homeless men and his lovely wife as well' we are truly Bless to have such giving and dedicated members here at Comfort Keepers Ministry. Well Pastor I am going to go get a couple of brothers to help me set up the tables in the hall for the luncheon.

Thank you my Brother, oh by the way when I was on the way here I seen something very strange, but maybe I was mistaken, so never mind just pray I was wrong. Okay, you sure? Is it concerning anyone I know Pastor? That's okay Brother, I might me thinking wrong, I am so sorry my brother to even allow you to see something was wrong, I just might need some new glasses, nothing to be alarmed about, close the door on your way out okay and thanks again for coming in to help set up for the brotherhood fellowship.

No problem Pastor Knight' I love doing the brotherhood it has grown so much since last year, well I am going to let you get back to making that wonderful meal for us, and if you need me I am down the hall. "Brother Devon walks away".

Lord I truly pray that my eyes were playing tricks on me because what I seen was not right and could turn a

Trapped: Earlina Gilford-Weaver

family upside down, well you know Pastor Knight is getting up in age Lord but you also gave Abraham awesome vision, let me stop talking foolish and finish making this peach cobbler the men are going to love this, I can say this myself I put both feet in this hum' hum'.

Trapped: Earlina Gilford-Weaver

Knock Knock
Chapter 5

"**Donna answer door**" Hey girl what is going on? Are you ready to go shopping?
Yes I guess' have you heard from Lisa? I thought she was riding with you.

No she did not call me yet' so I came right over, thinking maybe she came here, so did you decide on what stores to go too and the colors? Donna to planet earth' hello'...

Oh yes Carol I am so sorry, I really wanted Lisa here to be apart, Mother always thought we were against her adopting Destiny, so I wanted us to surprise her by planning this party for Destiny together to show her that we love that little girl just as much, when me and Donnie has her with us people think that's our daughter. She does look like you and Donnie I told you, your mother should of adopted Destiny for you guys.

Trapped: Earlina Gilford-Weaver

You know what Carol you said something right for once, but you know what girl I believe when I do have a daughter or son I believe our child will look just like that funny huh, but I want us to experience that together, let's change the subject, the way it looks now its best we don't have a child.
Why you say that?

Carol Donnie never came home last night, and I called Melvin to see if he was working late and he knew nothing about working overnight, so you tell me what's really going on, this is not right, I am so upset, now I am thinking did God really give me this man? Or was it just me?

What! Is he crazy? What in the world would make him stay out? Did you guys fight about anything?
No, and even if we did that is no excuse for him not to come home or call, I care less what happened, when one with us is mad neither of us should ever stay out all night especially a married man, I am truly feeling trapped in this marriage all by myself.

 Oh honey, it will be okay **"hug's Donna"** maybe a little shopping will put a smile on that face, I have a special

Trapped: Earlina Gilford-Weaver

place we can go, since you want Destiny birthday to be a special princess, I am upset myself with Donnie I truly do not understand
his behind at all, by the way is Charlene coming shopping with us? You know she is a big kid herself.

No I called her this morning and she said she has jury duty this morning, I will call Lisa on our way, I really need to get out of this apartment before Donnie gets home, I am not feeling any of his lame excuses so please let's go before I *"pause"* never mind let's go.

What say it, before you kill his black behind, wait a minute girl that's my new man Donnie is yellow, any way I will be your witness, I was watching murder that I wrote last night and wrote down some awesome Ideas of how to kill your man with a body missing for 100 years and you know Charlene is a cop and got our back so you got the clearance of the man just never came back home already, so we both can get the Insurance money the same day, how much policy you got on his butt?

Carol stop talking crazy, I am not going to kill anyone, much as my anger wants too, no one is worth me sitting in prison. Yeah you right we got to see how much the Insurance policy is worth first, because you would be

Trapped: Earlina Gilford-Weaver

crazy if you kill him and only got a $5000 I Hope life Insurance. **"Both walks out door"**

Later that night"

"Talking on phone" Hey man what you doing? Is Lisa anywhere around you? Alright' listen if Donna ask you anything about did we work over tell we did and when you left the office I was sound asleep okay. What when did she call? Then let her know that you made a mistake man' let her know you forgot I had to do that new project all night, and then went to the gym that morning, just clean it up man, get Lisa out your butt and think for a chance. Did you say anything to Lisa yet? Tell Lisa you messed up and you forgot, she will believe you, just buy her a new outfit man alright I got to go Donna walking in the door, **"hang up the phone"**.

"Walks in the door" Well I guess you decided that you knew where home was Donnie' where have you been all night? I have been up all night calling your phone and office have you listen to any of the messages I left? I just can't believe you did not come home at house who bed to you laid in or was it legs?

Trapped: Earlina Gilford-Weaver

Baby I did not want to wake you up, I lost track of time I had got a new project at work that took up a lot of time, Melvin was supposed to help but you know your sister so he left me hanging, I fell asleep and when I woke up it was 4P.M. and did not want to wake you, so I finished the project and then met Melvin at the gym he told me you had called him and forgot about the project, Lisa had his head in the clouds, and I would of called this morning but he told me that you and Lisa was going shopping for the surprise party for Destiny.

Yes I did go shopping at least I know where home was, and I talked to Melvin to see if you guys was working late since you never answered my calls, and he knew nothing about work overtime, he was acting a little strange like he couldn't talk, I just don't understand that. Melvin is not a person that would forget if you guys were at work, but I am glad you are okay, for a minute you had me believing something happen to you or you were with another woman.

Now baby come on, you know I love only you, and you are enough woman for me, I am working hard so we can have a great future, and maybe one day soon have them kids you always want, work is the only other woman that I will cheat on you with, so come on over here and

Trapped: Earlina Gilford-Weaver

give daddy some of that sweet kisses I missed all night, I missed my sexy sweet chocolate woman.

Did I hear you right Donnie "with a big smile" did I hear kids? I can't believe you said that Oh my God baby I am so sorry but you really had me so concerned and I was worried when you never answered any of my calls.

Baby I am sorry you was worried but where have you been all day and night? I know shopping did not take all that time; you were only shopping for Destiny right? Well I was shopping with Lisa and you know how she shop, she turned Destiny birthday into her fashion show, and I had to remind her that Destiny is only turning 1years old not 21, but we do want to make it very special to surprise mother with giving this party for Destiny since she thinks we don't support her for adopting a child and divorcing our dad.

Baby that is so nice, well anyway I got something I want to surprise my wife with so go put something on nice for your husband because I want to take you out to dinner. Oh baby that will be very nice to go out for a change, we have not done that since our honeymoon, maybe you need to work more late nights, if I keep getting this kind of treatment, Yes let me go change.

Trapped: Earlina Gilford-Weaver

Yeah you do just that and put on something real sexy and I will be waiting **"Donna walks away"** Donnie talking on phone" Yeah baby it worked' she brought everything I said, I will talk to you tomorrow sexy and kiss our baby for me, see you tomorrow.

"Two days later"

Donna girl are you okay? It is about time you called me back, I had to rush right over, soon as I seen your name appear on the Id caller, did you get any of my messages? I tried to call you for two days straight in the row and got no answer, what happened when Donnie came home Saturday? I thought you decided to carry out my master plan without me, got the check and went to the Bahamas without me; did you kill the man without me? Where is the body?

Girl Carol' no! It has only been one day and me and Donnie spent the day and all night together. It felt like he was a different man. The Donnie I first felled in love with. He took me to dinner, brought me some roses and this nice necklace and girl we made the best love all night and all this morning. I was not going to answer your call, my mother calls, or my sister; I was in heaven

Trapped: Earlina Gilford-Weaver

and did not want to come back down. Donnie was laying it down every which way I needed it.

Girl save that information for your ears only, but I am glad you are happy and okay especially Donnie, I guess if I stayed out all night, I would wine and dine tapped that butt roll it over, dive on top, under sideways too…

Carol, Donnie was working all night on a new project and I was worried about nothing, his phone had died and he left his charger at the gym the other day. He told Melvin to let me know where he was, but since Lisa had his mind messed up he forgot, plus Donnie said he just wants the best for me when we have our first child together' he wants to make sure we are financially set.

Girl what! You guys talked about having a baby? Now that is the smartest trick in the book, hmm maybe I need some lesson from Donnie.
It was not a trick Carol Donnie was serious and he loves me he proved that last night, this morning, and yes we did talk about planning for kids' it's like God answered my prayer right on time.

Trapped: Earlina Gilford-Weaver

Yeah I guess' or it was the knocking the hips all night that went to the brain, girl I thought you going to school for 12 years gave you some common sense.
Carol for real God does changes things; especially when you trust and believe, I just need to be more patient with my husband that's all and in and wait time. God timing it will work out. Well I guess I don't need a brother or sister talk. God beat me to it, let me call Charlene and tell her to turn off the siren and turn around the Insurance plot is over.

Knock knock: This must be Charlene now, Carol you are a hot mess, you know how fast Charlene drives, and I can't believe you told her that mess you made up in that brain of yours **"opens door"** Oh hello Mother, I thought you were Charlene.

"walks in" No' I am sexier, and better shaped then your freeloading friends, and where have you guys been? I have been blowing up your phones all night and all day, and you both were not in church this morning, so where is my son-in law Donnie? What did you do to him?

What are you talking about mother? And why do me and my husband need to be at your every beck and call

Trapped: Earlina Gilford-Weaver

all the time? Can't we just spend some time together alone, that is what married couples do?

I was just asking, because your sister Lisa told me Donnie did not come home all night the other night, and I know how your temper, it is just like Sam old drunk father you call a daddy, now where is Donnie what you do to him?

Well everything is okay Mother' and why is your focus all on Donnie when it should be on your daughter he was the one that stayed out all night, or did you forget' Donnie is out right now, and we are good thank you, and you need to stop talking about daddy like that, being a Christian woman in all, I am telling you Lisa has a big mouth.
Hello Mrs. McBride, you look very nice today.

Hello Carol and thank you, I always do, How are you and whoever his name is this week doing?

We are doing just fine and his name is Jesus' and me and the Lord is fine thank you.
Mother' that was not nice.

That's okay Donna' I love Mrs. McBride sense of humor.

Trapped: Earlina Gilford-Weaver

I am just saying, I am not hating at all, just look at me "**turning around**" Well I will check on you guys later, I was just checking on Donnie' I mean you both too see if you guys were okay.

Well thank you Mother, love you too, kiss Destiny for me, by the way me and Lisa have something we are planning for her, talk to you later on about it.
Bye Mrs. McBride.

It is Pat Dear, Pat' I am only a few years younger than you. "**Walking out door**"
Girl your Mother is off the hook.

Tell me something I don't know, Girl she acts like Donnie is her man, instead of my husband and her son-in-law, she seems to care more about him instead of me, maybe because he caters to her with them allowance checks to help her out with the house payments, ever since she adopted Destiny she need the extra help, since Daddy left her a years ago without any financially support.

Well we both need to pray for her, you know she loves you in her own crazy way, but I am glad about you and Donnie, I am about to leave so you and your man can

Trapped: Earlina Gilford-Weaver

finish making my Godchild, I only agreed to one child a girl so you can pass the rest on to Charlene.

Not today Carol we are planning for the future and in God's timing.

Did you look in the mirror when you got up, we are not getting younger, I mean you are not getting any younger, I was 10 years younger than you when we were in school, I was surprise they finally let you out the first grade at the age of 15'

Carol I am not playing with you, are you sure you are not my mother's child' **"hugs Donna & walks out"**

"Pastors Office Again"
Chapter 6

"One week later"
Hello brother Donnie "shaking Donnie hand" So glad you stopped by, I just want to let you know we appreciate all the clothes you donated to the men shelter, them brothers are walking around very sharp. No problem Pastor Knight, God has been good to me and this is my way of giving back, you wanted to see me? Is there something wrong? It sound like it was important on the phone.

Well my brother' in a way it is, but I could be very wrong, but I had to call you over so I could address this matter because it is something that has been bothering me for a while, about a week ago I stopped by a new member home to drop off some food from the food drive, and I was riding by Mrs. McBride house and seen

Trapped: Earlina Gilford-Weaver

a man that looks just like you kissing her, but his head was turned so I could not see his face clearly.

Now that's funny Pastor... real funny because what in the world would I be kissing my wife mother for? I barley want to kiss her on the cheek, now that is a laugh for this morning. But no way it was not me Pastor. I was not even in that area for over about a month now, I pray you did not mention this to Donna ?

No my brother I would never do anything like that without talking to the source first. I knew that was kind of crazy to ask but I had to make sure and get if off my chest and you have truly ease my mind a lot.

Very understandable Pastor, you have been with this family for years and I would have done the same thing, but good you know because that was a joke. I don't know who you seen but it was not me, maybe Mrs. McBride was getting her groove back??? Lord lets end this conversation it made me almost lost my appetite, just thinking about that. yes Mrs. McBride is sharp' but not my kind of sharp.

Sorry about that my brother. I just had to make sure, it was eating me up to even think that way and I have

Trapped: Earlina Gilford-Weaver

known that family for a long time, you have a bless day. **"Shake's Donnie hand".**

No problem Pastor, thanks for talking to me first, you have a bless day as well. **"Walks out office".**

Trapped: Earlina Gilford-Weaver

"Two Weeks Later" Donna & Donnie's Apartment

Chapter 7

Hello sis, what did you need to talk to me about that's so important?
Well sit down Lisa, this phone call I received will blow you away'
What call?
Daddy called and said he needs to talk to us concerning why he left, we have not heard from him in about a year I was in shock.

What! After all this time, this is crazy, where have he been all this time?
I don't know Lisa, he said he was out of town and he will be here Saturday, All I know is he said God said it was time for us to know the whole truth about why he left.

Trapped: Earlina Gilford-Weaver

The truth of why he left, I cannot believe he waited a whole year to tell us, wait a minute that is the day we are giving Destiny birthday party.

I know Lisa, that's what I need to talk to you about' I had invited him to the party.
What! Why would you do that? He does not even know about Destiny, and mother is going to have a fit. Daddy said he already knows about Destiny, and he knows it is her birthday. What, him and ma'am been talking all this time without us knowing, that's messed up? I truly cannot believe this mess at all. I truly do not believe this, he asked me not to tell mother that he is was coming, and he made me promise.

Why? Now that definitely sounds crazy, don't tell mother, now that is truly asking for trouble, you know how she feels about him Donna.
I know Lisa but I really don't know why he said that but he just said not to tell her because if she knew he was coming she would leave town.

That just sounds crazy, why would mother leave when she knows he is coming, it got to be something he is not saying, you need to call him now and let me talk to him.

Trapped: Earlina Gilford-Weaver

Lisa please don't say anything, daddy has been talking to Pastor Knight about it, and I know you, you can't keep a secret, and he said this would be the best thing for all of us, God would want him to tell the truth, so please don't say anything like you told mother about Donnie not coming home, after I asked you not to say anything to her.

What are you talking about? I never told her about Donnie not coming home, I would never betray our trust, but I will not say anything about daddy either, maybe he wants to get back with her that's why he talked to Pastor Knight, okay But since you pray all the time then you need to let God know that we need the cover pull off this whole situation and please tame mother.

Yeah I know she is like a ticking bomb ready to explode when you mention his name   but no one can know not even Melvin or Donnie Okay?
Okay, Saturday can't come too fast for me, I miss my daddy, plus he owes me a year of child support.

I miss him too, Lisa wait a minute girl you are too old for child support,
Well maybe fatherless support then, any way I want to hear why daddy left us and you know Mother acts like

Trapped: Earlina Gilford-Weaver

we were the cause, but we know that is not true. Daddy loves us, something bad had to happen for him to leave the way he did and never called and stayed away this long.

I know Lisa, God is always right on time, when we put all our trust in him and have faith as small as a mustard seed it can move mountains, just look we will be celebrating two things on that day, Destiny Birthday and Daddy coming home, just maybe we can all be a family again, if that's what God has in store for the McBride family.

Yes' that would be nice, let me go, I will talk to you later sis I need to go shopping
We just did the other day Lisa, didn't you buy enough? You are going to put you and Melvin in bankruptcy. Yes but that was before I knew daddy was coming, and this is why Melvin works for me dear sister love you. **"Hugs and Lisa walks out"**.

"Saturday, The Birthday Party"
Chapter 8

Well you girls have done a nice job on this birthday party.
Thank you mother, it was Donna that planned the whole thing, she wanted you to know that we support you adopting Destiny, believe that we love her as our very own sister, where is Destiny at anyway, I want to make sure she has on the outfit I picked out and her hair is still looking good, I paid that hair dresser too much money for her ponytail to look rough?

Oh Donnie has her, he wanted to take her and stop at this new kid store so she could pick out something special, he will bring her when everyone arrives. So she could be surprised and Lisa that outfit was to grown. My baby is 1 not 21 girl what was you thinking, she is not your Barbie doll twin. Well she is a McBride now' and that was nice of Donnie, He would make a good father

Trapped: Earlina Gilford-Weaver

one day, Donna must not know because she has been calling him all morning?

I don't know what your sister knows' and she needs to let that man breathe, it is not like he is committing a crime.

Well mother he is her husband, and he should let his wife know what he is doing? Plus she had already got Destiny an awesome gift from the both of them. **"Lisa walks away"**
What's wrong Lisa? Are you excited to see daddy today? Nothing sis, have you heard from daddy yet? When will he be here?
I really don't know, but Pastor Knight was picking him up from the airport.
"Pat walks over"

What are you girls over here plotting? You are looking to sneaky, it better be all about Destiny? Yes Mother, me and Lisa was just saying one year has gone by quick. **"Charlene, Devon& Carol walks in"** Hello everyone, Carol is here and now the Party can start, where is the birthday girl?

Ask my mother **"Lisa walks away"**

Trapped: Earlina Gilford-Weaver

She will be here shortly, and I hope them gift bags you have in your hand was not from both of you, my Destiny do deserve to have a gift from you both and I hope you both brought her something that would not break her skin out, my baby deserves the best' name brand only if you get my drift!

Yes Mrs. McBride, nothing but the best, I and Devon have gotten her a gift card in this envelope, so you can take her because she has so much and it was hard to pick out something. Very smart I guess they teach you some brain smarts at that police academy and my name is Pat, I am young enough to be your baby sister, and my, hello Brother Devon you are looking very sexy, I mean handsome today.

Thank you Ms. Pat you look very nice yourself.
Well thank you Devon, I see you have excellent vision, well the gift table is over there girls I will keep brother Devon company **"Donna walks away"**.

Hello everyone, thank you all for coming' you all look so nice
The place looks awesome Donna you and Lisa really did an awesome job, is Donnie here? Not yet Devon, I really don't know where he could be but I will be glad

Trapped: Earlina Gilford-Weaver

when Donnie get's here, I need him to supply the ice in the machine.

I know he is not working today, and where is the birthday girl? I want to see this outfit Lisa keeps talking about. No Carol he is not working, he said he had to do something early this morning and has not made it back yet, and the sitter will be bringing her soon, and I want Donnie here for the surprise.

What surprise? Girl don't worry Donnie will be here, and the place is nice.
Yes the place do look nice, Melvin and Lisa put up all the decorations, and thank you so much for getting and picking up the cake I got to go take a picture of it before everything starts. That is what friends are for, now, what is the big surprise? A male stripper?

Carol what is wrong with you? Why would they have a stripper at a one year old birthday party and at the church hall at that and Donna no problem me and Devon did not mind at all buying or picking up the cake we just had to keep Devon Jr from trying to get it. Look how big Devon Jr has gotten, he is looking more and more like you Devon .Well since Charlene did not mention

Trapped: Earlina Gilford-Weaver

my part I put in a $1.00 because her and Devon was .99 cent short, hater.

Well thank you all, no big deal Carol I know you would of did it all if I needed you too.
"Lisa runs over to Donna" I just saw Daddy get out the car with Pastor Knight he is coming and he looks good.
What your dad is here?
Yes long story Carol, let's be calm Lisa, where in the world is Donnie?
Mother did not tell you? He took Destiny to get something special.
What!

"Pastor Knight & Mr. McBride walk in"
"Lisa runs to her father" Daddy' they hug' I missed you so much tell me where have you been? Why have you not called us?
"Pat in shock and with anger" Who in the world invited this man here?
I did Mother, daddy wanted to be here' he missed us and called me a week ago.
For what! Too cause problems, or spread his lies again to you girls, because he did not know how to keep me, what in the world was you thinking Donna I know this

77

Trapped: Earlina Gilford-Weaver

was your entire crazy plan and betray me, because I know Lisa got better sense.

Ma please, don't start today, this is not about you all the time, he is our father and we miss him and want him here. It is okay baby, God is in charge today. I did not come to cause any problems. Man please' you care less about my girls and full of nothing but problems the day I met you and what do you know about God? You're an old crazy drunk just leave… this is my baby birthday party and I am uninviting you. This is Destiny day my child not yours.

Pat stop it, the lies stop's now, our daughters need to know the truth of why I really left, we owe them that much and it has gone on long enough. I will not let you destroy my family with all your make believe lies; because you are a weak, selfish, jealous crazy man. God is in charge that's why he ran you right out our life's.

Was it Pat? Tell the truth for once in your life, was it really God or was it you? You are just upset because you feel a little trapped now???
Ma, Dad please, this is Destiny day, please let's not make this about none of us, Daddy I know **you just wanted to be here for us today, and talk to his your**

Trapped: Earlina Gilford-Weaver

daughters about something important, but can we please do it with love and understanding and not with embarrassment on our family God is not please and we are still in the Lords house.

Well Donna then you should of thought about that before you invited the devil and I just bet he do want to talk to you both, all he want to do is mess up my life and have you girls against me like he always have with his lies that's all, I don't want this man here.

I don't like interfering in family personal situations but we all need to all pray and ask God for his hand and peace in this situation. We all are feeling overwhelmed by Mr. McBride presence, we cannot allow the enemy to win and come between a day that the Lord has made.

 Well Pastor Knight I believe it is a little too late for that now, you brought the Devil here with you today, so he has already made his presence known.
This is so crazy, my parents are acting like kids, ma let's just hear what daddy got to say before you judge him. He came here for a reason and me and Donna need to know why.

Trapped: Earlina Gilford-Weaver

Yes, I wanted us to talk before the party that is why I asked daddy to come a little early. But time is getting away and Destiny should be here soon so maybe you can tell us after the party. That would be fine baby but where is Donnie he needs to be here too when I do the talk?

I don't know, but he should be here shortly, but what do Donnie have to do with the reason you are here for me & Lisa daddy.
Mother said he took Destiny to pick up something special Donna which was very crazy since you have already gotten her something from the both of you.
What' he never said anything to me about that, I truly don't understand him doing something like that when we already got her something special together.

I would know why he has Destiny, and wanted to buy her something special.
What! How would you know daddy? when Donnie did not even know that he had planned to do that in the first place.

Excuse me everyone I know it is very tight in here, but would anyone like a drink of water, soda, Gin & Juice or a hit off my joint?

Trapped: Earlina Gilford-Weaver

That would be nice Carol, **No** I mean, what am I saying, this is no time for jokes, could you please just go and try to call Donnie for me again?
It is truly God's time for me to come and put a stop to all this foolishness, deceit and lies no telling what else has been going on.

Okay Sam McBride I have had enough out of you, leave now before I kill you myself "reach in her purse".

Ma stop it, you have truly lost your mind bringing that in the house of God "grabs Pat"
"Melvin Holds Lisa" Lisa baby let's take a walk so you can calm down.
I am okay Melvin; I just want to hear what my dad got to say to us after a year of wondering. Sorry everyone but I just got an emergency call from the station and got to leave, I will be back soon as I am finished and kiss Destiny and tell her happy birthday for me.

Baby come on I will drive you there and come back
Okay baby let's go, Donna I will be praying that everything works out.
Thank you Charlene and you guys drive safe.
Daddy' please tell us what it is, I want to know now.

Trapped: Earlina Gilford-Weaver

I know baby girl, well Donna I want you both to come over here and have a seat, I know I left you girls with a bunch of questions unanswered; but daddy is here to explain it all, I want you girls to know that I love my family. But there can be things that can happen that will turn a family upside down and apart, but through the Grace & Mercy of God unchanging hand to forgive us for all our short comings and wrong doing. We can find forgiveness through it all, and this is why I am here today I found that forgiveness.

Yes Sam I guess you did through all the drinking you put me through, and now you are here to poison my girls with your hateful lies.

You right Pat my drinking did play a part of my bad decision, but who lies and deceit that tore it apart? But no more, God has delivered me from the spirit of alcohol, so no more protecting the lies you have created. Go to hell from where you came from, I will not stand here and listen to this mess any more, and if my girls I created and carried for nine months and nursed for 18 years loved me they would tell you to go to hell too.

Family let's pray, Lord we need you right now, please fill this place with your presence in the name of Jesus!

Trapped: Earlina Gilford-Weaver

Let this family know that you are in charge to heal what is sick. Fix what is broken, deliver what is bond, Lord fill their minds with your peace and fill their hearts with your love. Free them this day from all the confusion that the author of lies has implanted. Lord let them know that this is really you Lord in Jesus that is going to bring the unity back in their life's in Jesus Name Amen. **"Pat walks away"**

Mother please don't leave, we love you and need you here to hear what daddy got to say.
Yes mother what do you got to hide that you don't want us to know? Daddy' please tell us now.

Would you guys like for me to leave?
No Carol you are family too, please stay, were you able to get a hold of Donnie yet?
No' not yet his voice mail keeps coming on.
Mother did Donnie say where he was taking Destiny?
No not really, but he knows what time to have her here. He knows that the party has started already 10 minutes ago so why is he not here yet? So daddy maybe we can talk now.

Let's all have a seat, well baby Girls I first want to tell you both how sorry I am for all the pain and heartache I

Trapped: Earlina Gilford-Weaver

have cost you. I love you girls so much and please forgive me. "Pause"... Lord give me the strength for what I am about to say, about A year ago in Sept. I went on a business trip you girls remember?
Yes daddy we do.

Well baby I came back early to surprise your mother and you girls, but I was the one that got a surprise. My whole life flashed in front of me. I could not believe what I seen.

Wait a minute daddy' I got married in Sept. and you left right after the wedding soon as me and Donnie got back from our honeymoon you were gone. So what are saying daddy? Was it because I got married?

No baby, let me finish, remember the day
 I came by two weeks to and surprise you with the dress. I had custom made for you from Paris and I asked you were you sure you wanted to marry this guy and you looked at me with tears of joy that I never seen in your eyes before with a glow and said daddy more than life itself and you asked me why was something wrong daddy? Well I was a coward on that day and I said everything was good as long as my baby was happy.

Trapped: Earlina Gilford-Weaver

Well I could not destroy my first born day with my hurt and pain.

What hurt and pain daddy?
Well baby this is hard for me to say, but I came home from Paris earlier to surprise my wife. Your mother and found her in the bed with another man.
What? Are you sure daddy? Not Mother, who was it? Did you know who it was daddy?
Stop lying… you old fool tell them what really going on! Tell them that our marriage was over and I was divorcing you, because Lisa and Donna were not your children and I was unhappy with you for years.

Pat stop with the lies, you will not cover this with more lies.
Sam you know we only stayed together for Donna wedding day. So her day could be special. What a mistake I made, I should have locked you up a long time ago when you hit me. Yeah Donna and Lisa your precious father the drunk use to beat me when he come home from drinking all night. Pat when are you going to stop with the lies. I never ever put my hands on you' tell your daughters who was in the bed with you the day I came home.

Trapped: Earlina Gilford-Weaver

Daddy' do you know who it was?
"**stands up**" Yes Lisa baby it was Donnie. But before you knew who it was I want you both know I had to come back after I had Donnie investigated I and found out some things concerning him too, so I want to "**Grabs his chest and kneel to the ground and past out**". Daddy what's wrong, Daddy, daddy, get the chair, hurry
Please someone get my father some water, get him some water hurry
Call 911, call 911 daddy, daddy
God don't like ugly, he was lying. So God stopped the devil, die… die… and take it back to hell from where you came from and going back.

What is wrong with you, my father is having a heart attack are you crazy mother, Donna let's get dad to the hospital quick, Mother get out the way.
The ambulance is on the way Lisa, Pastor Knight please lay your hands on him now, Lord' please help us right now in the name of Jesus.

"One Hour Later"
Chapter 9

I just cannot believe my daddy is gone, what happened? He looked good and healthy. What was he going to say mother before you starting attacking him it is all your fault my father is gone. Lisa it is no one fault please calm down, this is hard for all of us to swallow. Our father is gone and we need each other right now. If he's really our father you heard what mother said before she killed him.
Lisa no one is the blame the doctors said. Daddy heart rate was very low which means he had a heart disease.

Well mother tell us the truth now was he really our father? Is that what daddy wanted to tell us? Was the man he caught you in the bed with our father?
Lisa do not worry about that right now. I will tell you later, where is Donnie with Destiny? Carol did he ever come to the fellowship hall while we were at the hospital?

Trapped: Earlina Gilford-Weaver

No Mrs. McBride I help cleaned and gathered all Destiny gifts and bring them here. I tried calling his cell phone to let him know you guys were at Mercy Hospital but could not get through.

I tried calling him myself while I was at the hospital and all I could get is the voice mail
"Knock knock"
"Pastor Knight answer the door"
Where is Donna Pastor?
She is in the Kitchen room, **"Charlene walks toward the Kitchen room"** is everything ok Brother Devon?
No Pastor we really are going to need prayer.
What? Is it concerning Donny Devon?
Yes Lisa.
Well really it can be no worst then what we just went through our father just died an hour ago.

"Donnie & Charlene walking in the Living room" Why do you want me to come in here to talk Charlene? What's wrong? Why are you looking sad? What you heard about what happened to my dad?
I am so sorry to tell you all this but Donnie and Destiny was killed in a car accident this morning' they were not able to get in contact with the family, until I went to the

Trapped: Earlina Gilford-Weaver

station and told them I was close to the family, and let me be the one to come to you all this.
What! What are you talking about? There's got to be a mistake Charlene, maybe it was someone else.

No Donna it is true it was Donnie and here is the report they had Destiny listed as his daughter!!! What??? Destiny is not his daughter, why did they put this on the report? Wait a minute it was another guy in the car who is this they say a guy name Tony Whipple was listed as a passenger, is he dead too?

No he is in the hospital, the officer that was on the scene said before Donnie passed, he said his daughter was in the car, and the only other child that was in the car with him was your little sister Destiny, and Mr. Whipple and Destiny did not make it, she had suffered a bad head trauma, Donna I am so sorry.

What? What' did you say about my baby Destiny? No my baby can't be gone, where is she? Where is my baby? No no' no **"Pat runs out the door"**.
Oh my God, are you serious' this can't be happening, we just lost our father, he just died of a heart attack, sis please don't cry **"hugs Donna"** God where are you? where are you?

Trapped: Earlina Gilford-Weaver

This is my entire fault. I told daddy to come you all with this, got to be all my fault for inviting daddy here.

Donna this is not your fault. Please don't blame yourself for all of this. Lord we truly need your Grace and Mercy over my friends right now, this is too heavy.
Sister Donna and Sister Lisa do not blame yourselves for this. God did not allow this to happen for you to blame yourselves. I don't have all the answers right now, but the Lord will show his hand in all this and he will give you both all the strength to go through. Your father had called me several weeks ago saying he had to talk and to see his girls. He was sick and had a very bad heart disease and the doctors had given him 2 weeks to live. So he gave me letters and written will for you girls in case he did not make it here.

Did he tell you what he wanted to tell us? Maybe he is not our real father.
No Sister Lisa he did not only wanted prayer and guidance on what to do. I only knew that it was something that would change everyone's life.

I just cannot comprehend all this, my daddy, my baby sister and my brother-in-law, God please tell us why. It is going to be hard to do this. We lost a lot in one day.

Trapped: Earlina Gilford-Weaver

How can I call his name Pastor when my world has been turned upside down. I don't know where to start. I don't know what to say. I don't know what to think or how to pray. My husband, my father, and my little sister is gone and we are still here with all un-answered questions of why our father left. What was he going to say? Why did Donnie say Destiny was his daughter? This is a big blur spot in our life now.

Sister Donna In the mist of everything God is still on the throne and he sees all the pain. Tears and sorrow and just when you think you can't make it through, just hold your hands up and give it all to him. My God cares and he knows what we are going through just trust and believe, never give up. Never lose your praise. In the midnight hour God is going to work it out just give it to him and rest in his arms. Is there anything I can do for you girls before I leave? I truly need to go in a warfare prayer for this family and to see where Sister Pat ran off to she was not in her right mind.
Thank you Pastor Knight, maybe I need to go with you to find my mother, she ran out of here and I am very concern. Yes baby let's go and try and find her and take you home to get some rest, it has been a long day.

Trapped: Earlina Gilford-Weaver

No, Melvin I want to come back over Donna house. I don't want to leave my sister' she just lost Donnie, and she needs me here with her.

I will check on you girls tomorrow. Please try and get some rest you have a long Journey ahead and the letters your dad left me to give to you both I will bring over tomorrow. If you need anything tonight please call me at any time.

Lisa go and look for Mrs. McBride I will be here all night and every night for Donna I am not going to leave her, you both are going to need some rest.

Okay Carol, but sis please call me if you need me no matter what time or hour I am here, I am going to look around the neighborhood and at mother's house to see where she is at, I love you sis.

I love you too Lisa but Carol is here and please get some rest, Melvin please take care of my baby sister."**Minister Elliot, Lisa & Melvin walks out door**".

Carol what I am going to do without Donnie "**Carol Hugs Donna**".

"One Week Later"
Chapter 10

Thank you Pastor Knight for handling everything, the Home-going Celebration Service for daddy, Donnie and Destiny was so beautiful we are so grateful to you.
Yes it was; I was ready to re-dedicate my life on this morning! Donna would you like for me to put a pot of fresh coffee or get some refreshments for everyone?
Not for me, I am too wired up as it is, I am still full off the word and the food at the fellowship hall. what about you Pastor?
The same here no thank you Carol.

I just cannot believe our mother did not show up for the funeral at all, we have not been able to contact her or know where she is at all. Maybe she went to the Virgin Island to see Destiny real mother. I don't know Lisa; she loved Destiny so much that was strange for her not to be a part of the funeral arrangements. Maybe she was still

Trapped: Earlina Gilford-Weaver

mad at me for bringing daddy here and who was that guy at the funeral I never seen him before, he was truly broken up over Donnie death, but when I went to approach him he left.
I know that was strange Donna because he was not looking right at all. But you might be right maybe mother did go tell Destiny biological mother. But sis who would not be at a funeral for their own child and son- in law she adored so much and husband rather she like him or not. Not to even be there for us, I can't understand her actions at all, we need each other more than ever.

Well my sister's everyone deals with pain and lost of a love one different, but we are praying for Mrs. McBride strength and pray that God brings her home soon.
Yes we need her, and she needs us, no matter what our past was we have today and time is too precious to hold on to things in the past no matter what it is.

Praise the Lord on that my Sister Donna if only we had more saints that thinks like you, Well I the letter and the will of your father with me so that you both can read it if it's okay I will read the will of what your father left in the care of the church if that's okay with you both.

Trapped: Earlina Gilford-Weaver

Yes pastor that would be fine, you don't mind if he reads the will Lisa do you?
 No that is okay with me Donna.

I can leave if you all need privacy.
No Carol that's fine I want you to open us up in prayer. Of course Donna… could we all hold hands, Yes, Lord we are gather here together in your name, you say in your word Lord when two or three our gather in your name you are in the mist of it all. So help us to understand with the patience, wisdom and knowledge that only you can give, and lord keep our hearts open to forgiveness no matter what it is and give my sisters Donna and Lisa and their Mother the strength to move forward as a family. Lord bring Mrs. McBride home safe and with a sound mind and unite this family like never before in Jesus Name Amen.
Amen Carol, girl I am in shock' I felt like I was hearing myself pray.
Well Donna the word does let us know what we hang around we become, and I hang around the Lord in you.

And don't forget Carol you hung around me too.
I know Lisa, this is why I pray.
Ha, Ha, Ha, Sis you set yourself up for that.

Trapped: Earlina Gilford-Weaver

Whatever' you both know that I am still a working progress.
It is so good to see you girls laugh and smile, we'll let me start off with saying Mr. McBride was so proud of you both, that is all he ever talked about, his pride & joy, first let me tell you that in this will testament. Your father left you girls everything and his parent's church with me still the Pastor if that's okay with you girls.

Of course Pastor Knight, we would have it no other way.
I feel the same way' you have been our pastor since we could remember.
Thank you wonderful sister's I am truly honored, no one could fill the shoes of your Grandfather Bishop McBride and First Lady/Mother of the church you guys grandparents were so Anointed, that is where I received all my teaching and we all sat under the late great grandparents of the McBride's family, and he wanted the family home to stay with Mrs. McBride your Mother so that she could raise Destiny in the same home you guys were raised in, and the second Insurance policy would pay it off, he wanted everything to stay the same when he came to see me two week ago.
Wow after the way my mother treated him.

Trapped: Earlina Gilford-Weaver

Yes Lisa, your father had forgiven her, and set up a trust monthly income just for Mrs. McBride, because he said she was still his wife and God would have it no other way.
And I would like to give you both the letter he left for you girls, I feel you should read this since it is personal and address to you both. **"Pastor Knight hands letter to Donna"**.

Thank you pastor I feel that would be best for us to read the letter he wrote for us. I feel like we should read it, because it is more personal to us, so one of us should read it, if you don't mind Lisa. No sis you are right I rather for one of us to read the letter so you go ahead and read it Carol can we have this personal time together? I feel this is something me and Lisa need to do alone, if that's okay with you.

Oh no problem, I understand. Just call me later, see you Lisa, and Pastor Knight see you Sunday. Hold up Sister Carol I will walk out with you to give them some privacy, I will leave and give you too some time along. If you need me no matter what time or day it is call me and I will be right over and know God is working it out as I am speaking right now. So hold on to the will and strength of his understanding and not our own.

Trapped: Earlina Gilford-Weaver

We will pastor and thank you again so much for all you have done, keep our mother lifted up in prayer she needs God more than ever.
Call me as well Donna or Lisa you know I love you both as like you are my sister
We know Carol we love you as well, we will be just fine, call you tomorrow.
 Yes thank you both the best church family anyone could ask for. **"Pastor & Carol walks out door"**

Donna can you please read, I don't think I can without crying.
Yes Lisa. **'Donna opens envelope'**

The Letter
To My Girls, My Pride & Joy

Where do I start? Well God always said in his word to be honest with yourself first. So that you can Be true to others. So here it goes Donna & Lisa always know that daddy loves his girls and was very proud to tell the world that you both belong to me. I have always tried to protect you girl from any harm or danger, and sometimes your hearts but there is a time in our life's we can't do that and we got to allow God to take full control

Trapped: Earlina Gilford-Weaver

of the situation. Well Pride & Joy this is that time, this is the hardest thing I ever had to face and say that will not make our life's the same. I know because a year ago it changed my life.

Yes I was a coward to leave you with a big question mark, wondering why I left. What was wrong and never called or visit but there is a time in your life that you can only go and talk to God for the right answer. September of the year you were getting married Donna daddy took a trip out of town. I did not tell anyone where I was going because I wanted it to be a surprise. Instead the surprise was on me; I came home early from my trip and found my wife. Your mother in the bed with another man' my heart stopped and could not believe what I was seeing, not my love.

Not the woman I spent 39 years together, as the man turned around I wanted to kill him with my bare hands, but when I seen his face, the face that I would see every holidays and special occasions, my soon to be son-in-law Donnie, yes baby it's true, I found my wife of 27 years and your fiancé, now your husband in the bed together.

Trapped: Earlina Gilford-Weaver

"Donna hands began to shake and she drops the letter and Lisa picks it up and finish"

Donna and Lisa I should of told you both that next day, but how could I, when I came to you with the surprise I had a two weeks before your wedding day with the surprise designer wedding dress I had custom made from Paris for my first born to walk down the aisle as a princess. I overheard you talking to Carol that you never felt this way ever and how you could not wait to be Donnie wife. You went on and on. So I asked you baby do you really want to marry this man and you look at me with a look I never seen before with a glow so beautiful and said yes Daddy more than life itself. I said to myself' I could I destroy this day my daughter waited all her life for. So I did the worst thing a father could ever do. I allowed myself to walk my Pride, my first born walk into a man arms I despised and wanted to kill with my bare hands.

My pride Donna I could not deal with knowing you were with a man that would sleep with your own mother I been investigating Donnie and found out some things that you should know. I stopped drinking so I could come back with a level head and you girls would not think I was talking crazy. As time went on I could not watch you girls live this lie and started drinking my

Trapped: Earlina Gilford-Weaver

heartache away. But all I was doing and have done was destroy my life along with yours, Destiny is your real sister she is not adopted she is the child Donnie and your Mother conceived that night.

So like the coward I was I left and allowed your mother to continue to let you girls live the lie she created. I helped her do this. But Donnie is a Imposter he has a life style of a male gigolo, this is where his business money comes from he sleeps with men for money baby I have all the prove in my safe deposit box for you to divorce him soon as I received it I had to come and stop him from destroying your life baby.

Please forgive me and please forgive your mother and Donnie. Allow God to fix this. Do not try to handle or carry this on your own. I tried and it almost destroyed me. I love you Pride & Joy you girls are my strength please do not hate your mother she loves you. What the enemy meant for bad God will turn it around for his Glory. Let your mother know that I love her and I have forgiven her.

Oh my God Donna' this is sick. How could our mother do such a thing and daddy allow you to marry this dog and on top of this Donnie a male prostitute' sleeping with men' my God.

Trapped: Earlina Gilford-Weaver

Lisa God has already prepared me for this. I felt something was wrong the entire time, the way he was with mother and Destiny and he had to make sure she had an allowance every week. Before he ever took care of me; the concerns mother always had for Donnie and never wanted to sleep with me and this explains the strange guy at the funeral and in the car of the accident.

I know sis but Donnie and our Mother should have told you the truth. I am going to find her and when I do believe me she will regret the day she destroyed your life and Donnie better be glad he is six feet under but I want to stomp him 10 more.

No Lisa let it go it is all over now' no more lies. I am finally free from my doubt and fear of not knowing the truth. Even through when Charlene brought the police report over it said Donnie said Destiny was his daughter before he past and the strange name I never heard of before. All the late nights not coming home I felt it, I could not prove it, but I did pray for God to reveal it and he did.

Trapped: Earlina Gilford-Weaver

My God sis this is not right. We have lost so much. You lost so much, our father, a sister and you lost your husband, even though he was a no good dog I know you loved him and now mother because who knows where she could be.
Yes Lisa, but our mother lost more than we did.
What you mean sis?
I lost someone that was really not from God. It was my own choice, but we did not lose God and mother is lost she walked away from God when she did this and sometimes we reap what we sow.
Sis I am so glad I have you as a big sister, someone that I can truly follow and look up too. You have such an awesome forgiving heart. I am not there yet, I can't forgive her for this, and she should have died not daddy or Destiny.

Lisa never say that, we got to forgive her, so that God can forgive us for our sins and short comings. Don't ever let this hinder you from moving forward in God. No matter what our mother did she is still the mother God has given us.

I love you so much Donna
Me to sis, we will get through this. God please protect our mother and bring her home in Jesus name amen.

Trapped: Earlina Gilford-Weaver

Trapped: Earlina Gilford-Weaver

Six Months later
Chapter 11

Hello Lisa, about time you got your butt over here. Calling me screaming like you have got some awesome news to tell me and it probably a new outfit, so tell me what is the great news?

Well sis let's sit down I don't want you to faint.
What is it? Have you heard from mother?
No much better than that.
Girl what is better than finding our mother and you better not had spent all the money daddy left you, on clothes.
No sis.
Well what is it? Come on stop clowning.
Well sis Hum-mm.
Lisa come on stop playing.

Well yes in a way I have been shopping for a new wardrobe. Because I am pregnant

Trapped: Earlina Gilford-Weaver

What! Lisa stop playing, for real, you what? Say that again, I am not Melvin I am not buying anything.
Yes Donna, me and Melvin is having a baby.
Oh sis that is the best news I had all year, yes thank you God' about time **"Hug Lisa"**
 I know Sis and did you get your text back from the doctor yet concerning the HIV and Aids test.

Yes Little sister and you big sister is just fine clean board of health , so I will be here forever to spoil my niece or nephew and you just missed Precious she just left to go back to college her being home for them 3 weeks was such a blessing.
Well I am going to miss my smart intelligent niece. She's the Doctor in the family maybe she can deliver her new cousin.

That would be a blessing because she has 6 more months to go and she will a License Pediatrician Dr. Well you know she gets the brains from her Auntie Lisa. Okay Lisa, I let you have that one since you having my niece or nephew or both, yeah twins…

Knock Knock

Trapped: Earlina Gilford-Weaver

This must be Carol and Charlene because she called and said she had a surprise too, they are going to scream
"open door"
Hello, Charlene, where is your shadow? Carol
I don't know I thought she was already here and you are looking very exciting Donna. Hello Lisa you are looking like a glow on you.
Well Charlene we just got some good awesome news for once.
Well I have some great news for you myself.
What is it Charlene?
Well I continue looking for your mom, after 6 months and I found her.
Really' where is she? Where have she been all these months?
Hold on "walks to the door and comes back with Pat".

What is she doing here?
Lisa Baby please let me talk to both of you.
Come and have a seat mother, we have been looking for you, my God where have you been?
I was never looking for her and Donna how can you call her Mother after what all she did?
Lisa' remember what we talked about six months ago, she is still our mother, no matter what she did in the past, it is over.

Trapped: Earlina Gilford-Weaver

Well Donna I am going to give you guys some time along, and Mrs. Pat I will be back in a few hours to take you back okay
Thank you Charlene; "Charlene walks out the door"
I can't believe you are letting her be in your home Donna.
Baby please let me talk to you; I just want to say I am so sorry for all the pain and shame I brought to both of you,
You should be, but we are good we do not need you, we have each other.
I know you do.
Lisa please allow mother to explain, we got to forgive and you do not need to get upset right now okay, please do this for me.
Okay Donna for you, but where have you been all this time Pat?
Lisa I had to go away and allow God to fix what was broken in me, the things that had me bond had hinder me from being the woman of God and Mother and wife I needed to be, I can never take back what I had done, but I am asking for forgiveness from the bottom of my heart,

No you can't take it back because you had a child with my sister husband.

Trapped: Earlina Gilford-Weaver

You right and I have no excuses of why I did what I did, how I was raise or how I was not raise or what happened to me as a child, it gives me no reason why I punished my family for my past with my wrong.

God has given me another chance to get it right and I love you both please believe me,
Your action sure was hard to believe that, and I wanted to be like you what a joke.
Lisa please I need you to help me please sis, daddy taught us better than that and what we just went through has made us stronger so let's give mother a chance.

God is showing me how to really love, by loving myself first. I never told you girls about my childhood and why your grandparents were never in your life's, well I am ready to tell you now. I was 8 years old when my father would first start teaching me how to be a woman. By kissing toughing and having sex with me. My mother would just go drink herself until she would pass out so she could fade out my screams and cry for help. It would happen all the way until I was 16 years old until one day I met you girl's father and he knew something was wrong so he took me and we ran away to Vegas so that he could protect me. He got a job and married me, we never returned back here until I was 25 when his

Trapped: Earlina Gilford-Weaver

parents past away and Donna you were 2 years old, I promised myself that you both would never meet my parents. So I lied and told you both they were deceased when I was 8 years old and my grandmother raised me until she died.

Why I did the things I did to you girls were wrong, and I asked God to help me and deliver me from myself. I want to be a better mother & grandmother if you please give me another chance. Donna and Lisa I am so sorry please forgive me.
Mother you do not need to explain I have forgiven you the day I found out. I am glad you rededicated your life back to God and if God has forgiven you then who are we not to. I love you Mother no matter what and Lisa do too it is just hard for her okay?
Where have you been all these months?

And is dad our real father or was that a lie too?
No it is not a lie. He is you guys real father, I said that to hide from my own sins and hurt him for leaving and not forgiving me, but **baby** I had lost my mind the day everything happened and woke up in a mental hospital miles away. I don't even know how I got there. Or what my name was until a couple of months ago when God touched me and then Charlene found me.

Trapped: Earlina Gilford-Weaver

Why did anyone call us when they found out who you were?
Lisa I need Jesus Baby, so I only called on him until I was fixed, and ready to change so I could love me to love you so I could come to my daughters with my head up, and with a repenting heart, until then' I was no good even to myself.
Thank God for his Grace and Mercy, we serve an awesome God and a God of a second chance.

Well I want to know did you know Donnie was gay?
Yes your dad brought that to me one month before he came, but I did not believe him, I just thought he was saying that to get back at me for what I did.
Well it was true mother, Donnie was a male prostitute and I hope you got yourself checked.

Yes mother please I had too and I am just fine but would need to go back every six months for regular checkups, but I did get a report from a autopsy and he was clean but you never know since he had died and they cannot run a lot of test unless we resume the body, but know that I forgive you Ma, and I Love You, we are family, and through God's word we will make it

Trapped: Earlina Gilford-Weaver

And I guess if Donna can forgive you I can too and you can start by being a grandmother to your new bundle of Joy, I am having a baby.
Oh my God, Lisa' yes thank you Lord, Thank you, I love you girls so much. "Everyone Hugs"

The End!

When we put God in every storms, or situation he can move the mountains in any family, we can overcome all the OBSTACLE that the enemy brings up against us, no we should not betray the love for one another, but in the God word he let us know that even the very elect can fall.

So if you been through something that you feel you cannot forgive that person look at what the McBride family been through and say I can forgive too.
Be Blessed.

Trapped: Earlina Gilford-Weaver

Trapped: Earlina Gilford-Weaver

Pop Questions

What was Brenda Trapp she was feeling?

_____
_____
_____
_____
_____

1. Was Carol in her friend Donna marriage to much? If so why?

_____
_____
_____
_____
_____

2. When did you realize Mrs. Pat was having an affair with her daughter husband?

Trapped: Earlina Gilford-Weaver

_____
_____
_____
_____
_____
_____
_____
_____

3. Should Melvin told his wife that her sister was married to someone who was messing with men? Why?

_____
_____
_____
_____
_____
_____

4. Did Carol know that Donnie was gay before he dated her friend?

_____
_____
_____
_____
_____
_____

Trapped: Earlina Gilford-Weaver

5. Should Donna have known what was going one with her husband? If so why would you think so?

6. Was Mr. McBride right to come back and say anything since he allowed his daughter to marry Donnie? Why would you answer no or yes?

7. Was Lisa a good wife? Why?

8. Did Carol ever have a man? And who do you really believe she messed with?

_____
_____
_____
_____
_____

9. Should the family forgave Pat for all her deceit, lies? And do you believe if no one died would she ever told the truth to Donna?

_____
_____
_____
_____
_____

10. Ask yourself what happen in your life that made you feel that God was warning you but you felt trapped later and question yourself about?

_____
_____
_____

11. Who do you need to forgive so that you could move forward?

Trapped: Earlina Gilford-Weaver

Trapped! Was it Really God
Written By: Evangelist Earlina Gilford-Weaver & God
Gospel Stage can be ordered by contact: 330-423-9353
Web-Site   www.shekinahglorydrama.com
Email: shekinahglorydrama77@yahoo.com

Trapped: Earlina Gilford-Weaver

This Book Was Published By Maximize Publishing Inc.

MaximizePublishingInc@gmail.com
415-779-6297

www.ingramcontent.com/pod-product-compliance
Lightning Source LLC
Chambersburg PA
CBHW070203100426
42743CB00013B/3033